Copyright © 2019 By Greg Schumacher
All rights reserved, including the right to reproduce this book or portions thereof in any form whatsoever. For information, address the publisher at:
Greg Schumacher
14 Baldwin Rd
Scotia Ny 12302
Greg's Revolution Fitness
Gregsrevolution.com

Printed in the United States of America

First printing, 2019

Table of contents

Chapter 1 Perception Training — *Page 12*

Chapter 2 The Guide to the Healthier "YOU" — *Page 52*

Chapter 3 Wim Hof Breathing Method — *Page 80*

Chapter 4 Intermittent Fasting — *Page 95*

Chapter 5 The Workout — *Page 109*

Chapter 6 The Perfect Formula — *Page 125*

Chapter 7 Spirituality — *Page 131*

Chapter 8 Rest and Recovery — *Page 152*

Chapter 9 Let's Get Real About Food Choices — *Page 160*

Conclusion — *Pgge 165*

Greg's Revolution Fitness Goal is to bring you

Let's get started now!
I dedicate this book to the inspiration in my life, the one who came into my life and completed me, my soulmate Vicki.

Greg's Revolution Rules to Success

- Sing
- Dance
- Tell Stories
- Spend time by yourself
- See the magic in life

That's a good start… but why sing?

Our vocal cords vibrate. The world is made up of vibrations. Our vocal cords vibrating in a song like fashion actually unlocks happiness inside ourselves. Now stop being a pussy about it and sing!

I WANT A REVOLUTION!

Not a revolution you may be thinking, I want a self-revolution. A whole being revolution. I want us to get in shape, the mind, the body, the soul. The only way this happens is for you and me to look within ourselves and change the way we think. This book is all about YOU. The celebration of YOU. The transformation of YOU. Not to please other people, but to do it for YOU. So you can live the life you have always dreamed of. To accomplish great feats of self. To know yourself truly is to know the world. Let's get started on an adventure of a lifetime.

I Am Nature

I am not the missed call from my boss
I am not my dozens of unread emails
I am not my to-do list
I am not the likes on my Facebook profile
I am not the fast food I ate on my lunch break

I am
I am the leaves falling on my shoulders
I am the grass beneath my feet
The wind blowing through the trees
I am the water flowing between the stones
The soil in between my fingers
I am the choices I make

"Thoughts become things. If you can see it in your mind, you can hold it in your hand"
~ Bob Proctor

Forward

Gregory Schumacher: Greg's Revolution Fitness

Personal training as most people understands it focuses on one aspect of you – your body. I am not that typical personal trainer, though I used to be. I realized we are so much more than just our bodies. My methods are different because the whole you, mind body and soul, needs to be in tune in order to be healthy, in shape, and most importantly, understand what you really are. The outside result will be growing more muscle, shedding more fat, and having more confidence than you ever have. But the inside results, oh they are going to be fantastic.

Body: Effective
My physical methods apply wisdom and mental focus on your movements and exercises. I will teach and guide you so these movements will be almost effortlessly done.

Mind: Efficient
I will encourage you to continue learning, reading, and asking questions about everything you're interested in or trying to improve in, especially life.

Soul: Expansive
We can unlock great things inside our souls by being open to new perspectives and believing in ourselves. We can transform our entire lives by focusing our attention in positive directions. I will teach you how to do affirmations, visualizations, and guide you towards loving yourself.

Fist of truth

There exists a countless list of words many of us have attached negative emotional meaning to, as the rock sitting in the flowing water like a dam. Put your hand out in front of you and make a loose fist as if you were about to give a thumbs up. Rest it on your thigh or on a table in front of you. Now imagine there is a word written on it. This word could be any of those words with which you have attached negative meaning. It could be sex, spirituality, religion, fat, racist, girl, boy, drugs, food, punk, cancer, etc. Your fist represents the big rock sitting in the flowing river, which represents life. This word has been made a fact in your mind. This word you have attached all your fears, experience, and judgment to. When you encounter this word along your path you have judgments regarding the situation in which you encountered it. To be more specific you are preprogrammed from your past to now live with this word acting like a dam to your personal growth. You are not able to grow and expand in this area because you are convinced that your definition of that word is fact, when in fact it is just a word.

Take the word "sex" for example. As soon as you read that word you may have already had an emotional response which might trace all the way back to your childhood. You have attached facts and feelings to this word that may not be real at all. Are Bad memories, guilt, morality, power, or insecurity are all instant mental blocks to seeing the world clearly, to living in the moment.

Think about that fist in front of you with words written on it that you have attached so much meaning to. These words that do not give you a chance to have an opinion in this moment, they bring back the past like a sledgehammer.

These words cause anger, depression, stress, hurt, overreacting, and a storm inside you. If you can recognize these words and call them out for who they are you can begin to work through the things that haunt you. You can begin to move forward in your life in these areas that may take years of therapy. You can have freedom and live in the moment of life, not in the past.

In this chapter I will be presenting something called perception training. This exercise will help you rewire your brain to bring clarity and a different way to look at things in your life. This exercise will also help you determine these words you have on your life that reveal the Fist of Truth. Those words that are attached all the way back to your childhood. Pay attention to your emotional body as you make your way through this perception training.

Perception training is a method to rewire your thoughts about everyday subjects by using short essays to explain concepts in new ways. It will start triggering in your mind a world of different possibilities. Some concepts you already may have encountered. Please take the time to absorb these concepts one at a time. Ask yourself how the different possibilities presented make you feel in your mind and your heart. Remember that it is okay to challenge yourself and change your mind if need be. To change the way you live, think, speak is a very big process and takes bravery, but so rewarding. Good luck!

Chapter 1
Perception Training
"The moment you change your perception is the moment you rewrite the chemistry of your body"
~ Bruce Lipton

Be In the Moment

Being fully present in the moment is difficult in our modern world. Cell phones, television, social media and electronics distract us everywhere we go and we are conditioned to want instant gratification.

However, if you can master being in the moment in your daily life, you can master it anyplace. A story: A Buddhist monk went to a monastery in the mountains to find enlightenment. He sat in silence for months. He ate very little. He was completely isolated. He meditated and meditated until finally, he found enlightenment. He was free! Soon, his visa renewal forms arrived in the mail. He had to travel to town to return the forms. When he arrived at the office, there was a long line.

He waited and waited until finally it was his turn and he went to the window. The clerk looked at his forms and said: "I'm sorry sir, you're in the wrong line, the correct line is over there." He looked in the direction she pointed
 and he saw it was an even longer line. He screamed "Ahhhhhhh!" And enlightenment was over.

So you see he escaped reality to find enlightenment. In doing so it was not sustainable. He never went through the experience of growth in his usual environment. You must master being in the moment in all you do. Meditate in all you do. Whether you're sweeping the floor, washing the dishes, or taking a shower, find peace in the action. Find yourself not thinking about where you have to go, what you need to do in the coming hours. Just be.

Awareness

Awareness goes hand-in-hand with being in the moment but has more depth. It's the realization that there are no ordinary moments. Each moment we live through has so much to experience, but our brains can only process a fraction of the information around us. What you choose to focus on is what you see – like attracts like. If you focus on negatives, you will see and live a negative life. If you focus on the positives, then you open paths that will be amazing. Awareness also includes gratitude. Be grateful for where you are, and appreciate the world surrounding you. Try observing treetops - they have an aura just above them if you look closely. Feel the breeze and really listen to birds chirping. Be aware of what rain feels like when it falls on your skin. Appreciation of the world around you can bring you to a stress-free meditative state.

So, open your awareness beyond your everyday actions. Truly observe where and how you live.

Do Not Believe Everything You Are Told

We are bombarded by messages from others telling us what is good or bad for us, what we need or want, what we should do, and what we should believe in. Others want you to believe what they believe because having others agree with their viewpoints defines their identity. If you prove them wrong or go against what they say, it hurts their identity. You now internally force them to look at themselves in the mirror. What I am asking of you is to question everything. You have lived until now perhaps always being told to follow the rules and not to question them. We have every right to question the rules, but we tend not to as we have built boundaries within and live within them. Question the rules and break the walls down. Understand we have made ourselves powerless inside our fenced in little life yards. Empower yourself to question everything and find your own answers. Trial and error are okay. Failure is a learning experience! We fail in this life in order to learn about who we are. Failure is a great gift that we fear but ultimately it is how success happens. Failing is winning - it is a transformation if you allow it to happen.

Yoga

Yoga has existed by some estimates for 10,000 years. There is a reason it has remained in practice for so long. Yoga is not just an activity for stretching and balance. Yoga movements are not random. They were specifically assembled to contribute to the transformation of being. It is a great way of finding the balance of mind, body, and soul. This is the biggest reason I fell in love with it. Being a personal trainer, a college grad for physical education, and a fitness guru, I tried so many different sports and activities in my time. I always loved bodybuilding. It was fascinating to me how the exercises molded and shaped the body. However, when I found spirituality and eventually became awakened, I could not find an activity that satisfied all three perspectives of mind, body, and soul until I tried Yoga. It really helped me design and discover myself, combining muscle and fitness with the mind, body, and soul experience.

The Universe will not hand it to you

This is another behavior that we have been taught. You must feel like you are earning something to feel like you deserve it and we must keep chasing something so as not to lose it. I recommend keeping this in mind if you find yourself obsessing over a want. Understand the universe does not just drop what you want right in front of you exactly when you want it. It knows you will not appreciate it as much as if you had to work for it. Just remember in all your actions, expansion is your purpose in obtaining your goals. Do not grow frustrated by what you do not have. In fact, appreciate the things that you are blessed with, this mindset will bring more of the things you desire your way. Most of the time we focus so hard on the things we don't have, that we miss out on our lives, we don't enjoy what is in the now, and we push away the very things we desire.

Rebellion

Rebellion presents us with so many of our best experiences in life. Conformity does not offer new life experiences. If you yourself always followed direction and did exactly what you were told to do, you would cease to know your true self. You would lose your individualism. Often, rules are made to keep the masses compliant and are not based on any real laws of nature. Therefore, I think some social rules are meant to be broken and we are meant to push limits. You are meant to be different from anyone who has ever been here before or ever will be here. Be proud of all of what you are and feel. Do not try to conform and fit in. Just be you - this is the master plan all along. Your true self will expand the world.

Soul Mates

We have a natural tendency to assume that remarkable chemistry between two people is confirmation that they are meant to be together. In the heat of profound feelings, it seems counter-intuitive to imagine ourselves separate from a person we have determined is our soul mate. However, chemistry and longevity of the relationship are not necessarily the case here. Simply because we feel earth-shatteringly alive with someone presents, does not mean they are supposed to be our life partner. They may have come for very different reasons; perhaps to awaken us, to expand us, to shatter us so wide open that we can never close again. Perhaps they were sent from afar to polish the rough diamond of our soul before vanishing into eternity. Better we surrender our expectations when our soul mate comes. This person may just be coming into your life for a short time, like a drop-in visit. Also, soul mates do not have to be a sexual partner. They could be in friend form.

Remember, when you have the privilege and opportunity to have a soul mate in your life, it does not mean happily ever after in romantic terms, or life-long friendship;

it means tremendous growth of self. Your soul mate makes you look into the mirror and challenge yourself.

This person introduces emotions you maybe never have felt before. You feel it when you've found one, and there could be multiple in your lifetime if you are lucky! Life is all about expansion and no other better person to do it than your soul mate.

Wim Hof "Iceman"

Through the wim hof method we think outside the box of how to exercise the body from the inside. We strengthen the core bits. The cells, the capillaries, the heating and cooling system, the immune systems, the nervous systems.. Through this method of breathing, shocking the body using cold water and building a strong metal connection to the body we transform ourselves into happy, healthy and strong.

Meditation

I will get more into meditation later on in this book so this is a brief overview. Meditation also does not have to be a long drawn out process. It can be done in 10 minutes with great effects and is such an important part of growth. Meditation reduces stress which your body and mind will thank you for. Meditation is a way to connect to your higher self. Meditation brings clarity to your life goals and helps you focus throughout your day. Take the time to learn the exercises and lessons in the chapter on meditation for more discussion.

Masters Are Not Born, But Built

It is not uncommon to mistake a Master to be perfect person that lives effortlessly without growth or struggles. With that mindset we limit our own thinking to infer about ourselves that we could never achieve to mastery-level accomplishments in our own lives. Instead, we need to constantly be empowering ourselves by opening our minds to great possibilities within us. People around you may tell you cannot or you should not. If you ignore all the negative feedback from others and change your negative self-talk as well, your path to mastery of anything will be available. You will be able to achieve being a life warrior. Keep in mind, that to be a master means to be in control only of yourself, never of others. If you watch a Jiu-Jitsu master perform, it is like watching an artist. Every move is clean, seemingly effortless. At the end of a demonstration, the master is not bent over trying to catch their breath, but in full control. He also worked for many years to achieve his skills. He has wasted no energy and was efficient and focused. This is how I want you to approach life – encourage yourself, avoid wasting energy, and allow yourself to achieve mastery in whatever you choose.

Fasting and Intermittent Fasting

For thousands and thousands of years, we humans survived on a fasting diet. We were hunter-gatherers. We would go long periods without eating, then find food and eat like a king. Our bodies evolved to be like this, to survive like this. We are built to fast. That's a big reason why we are so unhealthy in this country right now. We eat waaaaay to often. Our bodies never get a break from digesting. Our bodies in the unfed state do some amazing things. All kinds of myths exist telling us we shouldn't fast. We shouldn't miss a meal. Remember think outside the box of conformity. Try things. Our bodies are our own doctors. Fasting has been around for thousands of years. It's what we are meant to do.

Be a Powerful Life Warrior

In all you do, keep in mind you are powerful. One of the strongest affirmations you can repeat is "I Am…" Repeat to yourself, "I Am Powerful". The reason behind remaining powerful is because when an individual chooses to be a victim, that person becomes enslaved to negative emotion. We lose control of our lives and lose sight of our goals. We become distracted by the things that make us feel powerless. We stop noticing the patterns of nature and nature's power. We neglect the power of our own energies and ignore the mind-body-spirit connection. "I Am Powerful" will bring you back in control. The only thing in the world that you can control is yourself. How do you want to shape your life? What experiences would you like? Know how strong you are, no matter what is going on in the world around you and use that strength to focus on the things you want. Build your energy up that you receive from the universe, from Mother Earth, from Father Sun. Do not let yourself get brought
 down the negative energies, be it gossip, bullying, drama, or sensationalized news. Avoid and find a way to shield yourself from these things. Raise your vibration levels by saying "I Am Powerful". I call this being a Life Warrior.

Start Living

It is not uncommon for people to spend their whole lives waiting for the perfect time to start living. They are afraid to be open to the possibility of failure, of finding their true passions, and of being unique. We are meant to be something and you will never know what that is until you take a risk. We have a drive inside for a reason! Death is not to be feared; what is to be feared is never living your best life during the short time you have on Earth. I want you to tap into your potential. We can find it together, and it will have you trying new things and falling in love with yourself.

Be Comfortable Being Alone

I will not try to convince you to be alone for your whole life. I will try to give you the gift of enjoying being by yourself and understanding you do not need anyone else to complete you. You are everything you have ever needed. Most people are seeking a partner their whole lives to complete them. As the seeker, you may manipulate your partner to fit your ideals. It is not fair to your partner to be your savior. In almost all cases a relationship build on those grounds will fail. Millions of people are unsuccessful in their relationships, in marriage, and in dating, because it is the relationship with themselves that they should be seeking. The greatest thing with falling in love with yourself is that you stop feeling desperate. When that happens, you can begin attracting complimentary, positive people in your life. When you do find a partner, you will no longer be putting pressure on your mate to be a superhero. Each person can genuinely be themselves and can accept the other for exactly who they are and relate in harmony. These will be some of the riches relationships you have ever felt.

These are the relationships that will evolve and expand you. These relationships will raise your vibration levels. The experience of falling in love with yourself will be the greatest gift you have ever received. I am going to bring this to you. I will show you the steps, the perception to start heading in this direction and be able to sweep yourself off your own feet.

Happiness

I witness a lot of people every day who seem never to be happy. They complain constantly or have a sense of entitlement as if the world owes them something and it has not paid up. If they do not get what they want they suffer and even if they get exactly what they want they still suffer. People have been brainwashed into thinking getting every desire will make them happy. In reality, they do not believe they are worthy of being happy. They trick themselves into believing they need to suffer more before they can be truly happy as if somehow you survive through many stages of suffering there is a rainbow at the end. For example, I had a friend that I grew up with, in the spiritual sense. We were both in our 20s. We would grow at about the same rate and were excellent facilitators for each other in the understanding of one's self. We read books, watched movies, did meditations and mantras. However, one day I kept growing and he stalled. I continued on my journey of self-discovery but he did not because he had the mindset that suffering was his answer. He would sit in his room for days upon days isolating himself from the world and became depressed instead of enlightened.

I, of course, tried to help him rise out of this, but he truly believed he needed to suffer more, and to this day he still does. Suffering is an illusion. It is a faulted sense of self. There is a place for it in growth but only a small part. True happiness comes from perspective. From understanding no matter what the outcome of any situation, you get what you want or you do not, either way, you are an extraordinary being.

HIT and HIIT Training

I have tried all types of training. I played football for a number of years and was a basketball ball player for a very long time. I also ran track and studied yoga. My main fascination has always been weightlifting. I am intrigued by building the body and molding it like a sculpture. I always thought what an amazing gift to be able to do this and I have been in awe of this my whole life. I never wanted to be big and bulky because I wanted to keep my agility and speed. For a while, I fell into the trap of thinking supplements were the answer to building my best body. However, supplements are ineffective in most cases, and only produce temporary results if they work at all. I've spent thousands of dollars on various products that guaranteed results. I did experience slight results at the beginning of a course, but in every case, sustained effects were not the result. Hopefully, I can save you some trouble and you can learn more easily where I learned the hard way. Remember, your body is a very awesome tool. If you feed it right, give it the proper training and rest, and bring mental positivity you can achieve almost anything. Your body will respond in fantastic ways!

The best part is that your results will be long-lasting. I truly believe in High-intensity training and high-intensity interval training. These methods whip the body into shape. Physically, your body has no choice but to react to short 20-30 sec rest periods between sets. You work very hard for 20-30 minutes only. Later in this book, I will bring you through this program in more detail.

Find the Zone

The zone is the state of concentration where time seems to slow down, stress is low, and breaths come evenly and easily. Athletes know when they are in the zone. Their focus is outstanding and the slowing of time is palpable. The athletes stop questioning what will be their next move. They are fully invested at the moment and they forget any mistakes they have made. They are razor-focused on their goals. The zone is built on total confidence and belief in one's self. It is the alignment of mind, body, and spirit. Amazing things happen in the zone. Your energies are vibrating in such a way that the impossible becomes the norm. This is the state I want you to strive for as often as possible in your physical training. Allow your intuition to guide you. Your training experience will be holistic; personal evolution and expansion will take place.

Get Rid of Your Bathroom Scale

The ubiquitous bathroom scale has long been viewed as the best tool to measure your physical fitness. In reality, the scale has little to nothing to do with how much progress you are making! Understanding the human body and molding it into a beautiful physical shape has little to do with losing weight in absolute terms, but in some cases gaining weight. Muscle weighs more than fat! So if you shed some body fat, and put on lean muscle on, you may maintain your weight or even gain weight. But, you look and feel better and experience a higher metabolism. When you add muscle to your body, your body burns more calories throughout the day. How should you instead measure your progress? First, build your self-confidence. Be positive to yourself with motivational self-talk. Next, take pictures after each workout or every other workout. Practice your favorite poses. You'll start to see over time you are making fantastic progress! Lastly, notice the sensations of being inside your new body. You will feel more agile, lighter, and more energetic. The stairs at the office will feel easier. Your posture will improve.

Just stay away from that scale and let your body and your body alone show you the progress you make!

Fat is a Great Energy Source

We have been told a low-fat diet is a healthy diet. However, human beings were never meant to eat man-made carbohydrates and sugars that tend to replace natural fats in processed foods. Pasta, bread, gummy worms, high-fructose corn syrup, cereal, and fast food are full of simple carbohydrate. Your body is not set up to digest this kind of food. Sugar is as addicting as heroin. Bread and pasta turn into sugar. Anything with high fructose corn syrup is caustic to your internal organs. Protein, non-hydrogenated unprocessed fat, fruit, and vegetables have always been humans' diets since we were first evolved on earth. Stick with that rule of thumb. Do not be afraid to eat fatty meats and whole eggs. Your body is designed to use the fat as your main energy source if you avoid simple carbohydrates. Enjoying fruit, but not too much to avoid eating too much sugar, green fresh veggies, eggs, meats, and fats, with very little carbohydrates will make your body feel great. Count carbohydrates, but do not count calories. I will tell you why later on in the chapter about diet.

Become a closer

I've never trusted people to do what they say they will do., because most people in this world are not closers. They don't finish what they start; they don't live what they dream; they sabotage their own progress because they're afraid they won't find what they seek I want to teach you to finish. I want to teach you to gift the world with the talent you have inside. To dream big and get big results. To say you will write a book. To write a book. All along the way telling everyone you are writing the best-selling book. It's called confidence and creating the world to give you what you dream. You must understand we have spent most of our lives down talking ourselves. Stepping on our own throat and checking any hope of success right out of ourselves. Why? Because we are scared. Scared of success. Scared of others judging us. Scared of losing ourselves. Scared of change. It's time… It's time for you and me and everyone on board to rise! It's time for our gifts from within to shower this world. We were born to make a mark on our time here. It's time to create our path to success.

Acid Reflux and Indigestion

For years, I suffered from Acid reflux and indigestion. My daily routine to find of comfort was handfuls of antacids and a prescription an acid reducer. I never had complete relief, often experiencing days on end of nausea, pain, and sleeplessness. Then I began researching and changing my diet. Finding a simple digestive enzyme, you can take during meals. They aid your digestion very naturally. Thus, us a good way to start. You can find them on Amazon. Next intermittent fasting is a miracle. It gives rest to the body from digestion for 16-18 hours. This is how the body is supposed to function. Feeding every 2-4 hours makes your body overwhelmed. Overtime problems start creeping up. Until you are in the doctor's office. Taking pills. I hate pills. I think there is no reason we should be medicated. Our bodies are our doctor. We just need to let it for its thing. By allowing your body to rest through a 6-8 hour eating window. Your body now can breathe. It can clean itself. It can reset. Daily.

Other things that help:
Low sugar diet
More fat and protein, fewer carbs.
Positive mindset
Less stress more fun
Apple cider vinegar and baking soda in a little bit of water mix one teaspoon each. Works like magic on an upset tummy.

The Universe and Everything in it is Energy

The structure of the universe is built on energetic vibration. Humans are vibrating beings. When we feel good, we vibrate at a higher frequency. When we feel bad we vibrate at a lower one. Through meditation, positive attitudes, and perspective on life we can raise our vibration levels. From a raised vibration level more great opportunities open up for us.

- We reach our goals much faster.
- We raise our awareness levels.
- We are healthier.
- We attract into our lives the things we want around us.

The same is true if you are negative, moody, or depressed. These states lower our vibration levels and we see things going wrong. We attract negative events that work against our goals and create obstacles. Remind yourself that it is all up to you and that you are in complete control of how you view the world. You can choose to see negativity and tragedy, or you can see this world is designed for positive experiences. These events that happen are for growing and learning of who you are. As you look it is created.

All the Greatest Achievers Were a Little Crazy

When you start transforming your life, you will view and approach the world differently. You may find yourself a bit isolated because people do not understand the path you are on and how you see life. You will begin to see patterns of the circle of life. How we repeat the same problems over and over throughout a lifetime just with different people/situations. When you think outside the box, others tend to find your views unusual. You will start to see that the information you are feed from formerly trusted sources is not necessarily true. Einstein, Newton, Da Vinci, Jesus, Buddha, Steve Jobs all saw the world differently. They saw opportunities and places people were not willing to acknowledge. They showed the world the impossible and experienced negative feedback in many ways. Remember this when your journey is not always easy. The things you will want to talk about with others around you may not be accepted or easily understood. You may want to show others your viewpoints, but some will not be interested until they find their own answers.

 But keep your heart open and you will find a few new people who will magically appear in your life that you can share with and go on the journey with.

Embrace Your Faults

We tend to look at elements in ourselves that do not conform to norms as faults. We hide our individuality and uniqueness to blend in with the pack. You are not to blame for this; it requires a lot of bravery to be completely outwardly unique. If you are one of the lucky ones who finds it in their heart to show the world all that they are, a wonderful thing happens. Remember, like attracts like, so that unique person begins attracting the people into his or her life that supports and compliments that individual. This is the main reason why so many people feel lost and alone. They simply are not showing the world who they are, so they attract incompatible mates. Also in showing the world your true self, you will eventually feel confidence, freedom, love, acceptance, and direction in your life. Finding your passions and goals follows direction. You will find happiness, not because of objects or accomplishments, but because you are alive. You can celebrate being all those things you thought were faults but realize our gifts and strengths.

Nobody has the gifts in such a way that you do. And the more you show them and are proud of them, taboo or not, there are people out there just like you, waiting to share the same thoughts and gifts.

Present the world the true individual you are. Show the world what a gift you are. You have these gifts for a reason, so show the world why.

Forget the Guilt

If you have guilt for minor mistakes and transgressions, accept your actions, and move on. There is no need to dwell on those feelings; you did your best to the best of your ability. Guilt is not a constructive emotion if it only brings you down. If you do not disengage from the past, you cannot move forward and grow. Develop the understanding that you can not change anything in the past. You can only change yourself in the present moment. This moment is the only thing that is important. This moment is where you are alive. The past is dead. You can certainly learn lessons from past experiences. Learning lessons and holding on to guilt are two completely different ideas. Right now, you can reflect on your actions in the past, and then decide to develop greater compassion for others, love yourself more, and learn to think about your desired outcomes before acting. Remember your awareness at that time was not the awareness you hold now. Life is a continuous learning experience. Treat it that way.

Create the Best You

The only way to repay the universe for this spinning globe, the ever-expanding forward supply of food and water, free oxygen and sunlight is to be the best person you can be. The only thing you owe the universe for these wonderful gifts that are taken for granted every day is to be the best you possible. I want to help train you to be the best you can possibly be. I want all three aspects of mind, body, and soul balanced and nourished to be the best you and repay the universe to the best of your ability. I also want you to understand that you owe nothing to anyone else. Just be grateful for what you have - your unlimited potential, energy, passions, and accomplishments; even those yet to be seen. It is not a question of if, but when.

Reverse Pyramid Training

There are so many different ways to train the body, I have found in the last year or so that lifting my heaviest set first has worked fantastically in growing and strengthening my body. There is science behind it, why I'm having the success with this, basically, it forces the body to call on a lot of muscle fiber recruiting because of the heavyweight first. You also mentally put all you can into that first set because you know that will be the heaviest one. Instead of the typical weight workout of saving heaviest for last. I always write down my results every session and try to gain more strength everytime I do that routine again. And it has worked perfectly.

Who Are We?

Underneath the superficial self, who pays attention to the banal details of day-to-day life, there is another self. The more you become aware of this other self the more you realize that it is inseparable to everything around you. In knowing this, you will see that you never die. The experience you are having that you call everyday consciousness, pretending you are not it. It is all in the eye of the beholder. You see what you want to see. It is in perception that you create sensations of; cold and hot, light and dark, good and bad. Our skin is soft makes wood hard. The wood is only hard in relation to soft skin. We evoke out of this whole universe; light of the sun, hardness of wood, sounds of laughter; just because of who we are. You are the creator of duality. You bring to life this world with perspective. You bring life to this world with experiences. You bring life to this world by facing your fears. You alone expand and explode the universe into growth. Be proud. To achieve your dreams. The universe cannot wait.

Chapter 2
The Guide to a healthier "you"

"Mindless exercise on fancy equipment cannot possibly achieve the desired results that two simple dumbbells or a barbell in the hands of a master can produce"
~Iron Guru" Vince Gironda

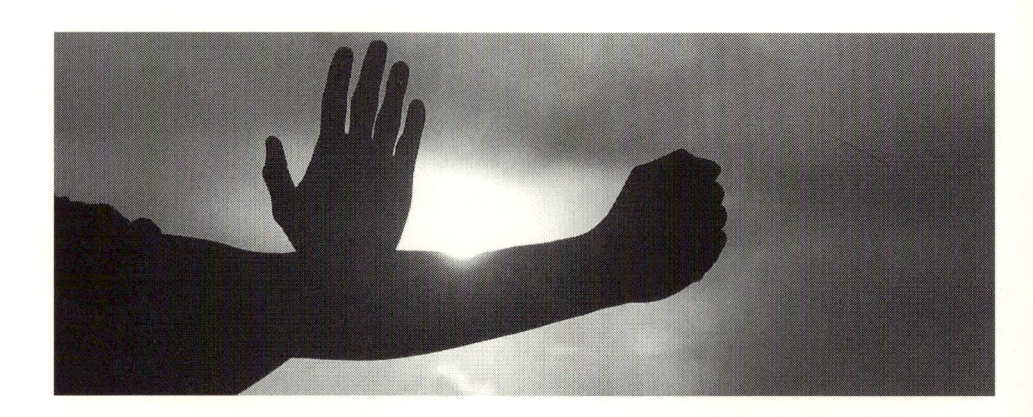

Guide to the Heathier "You" program

Yes, it is possible! You ask what is possible Greg? I say building muscle and strength at the same time shredding fat off the body to create the modern-day Hercules. To strengthen the outside and inside. To find love for who you are and what you do. To bring clarity to your life and purpose. To ward off disease and sickness. To show you your true potential. To bring you the feeling of being a Greek God like Hercules. This is something most of us can do. If you follow this program I'm about to lay out for you, it will be simple.

Let's make something very clear…it all starts with two words: consistent and persistent.

My first secret is a little thing called intermittent fasting…

intermittent fasting is the best thing to ever happen to me and now you. It simplifies your life and eating. At the same time, it allows the body a break from digesting, allowing your body to do miracles. Transforming the body into a growth hormone environment. This not only strengthens the exterior looks but internally you become superhuman. Your immune system, cardiovascular system, and cognitive self become clear, healthy and better than ever.

Why Fasting Works

Let us talk about why fasting works when other diets don't. If you want to know every detail and inner working look up Dr. Jason Fung, an authority on this subject.
 Think of the body as a refrigerator. On one side you have your daily food. It's 40 degrees. Milk, cheese, yogurt, veggies, etc. They are accessible and easily taken out and eaten. On the other side, you have the freezer. In order to use the freezer stuff you usually need to plan ahead. To thaw it out. No easy access. Not easily used.
Well, this is an example of what's going on in your body. The things you eat every meal is your refrigerator side. Easy access to the body. The body uses what it can. Then sends the rest to either waste or storage. Storage being the freezer part, extra fat on the body.

refrigerator side = the food you eat
Freezer side = the food in storage (fat on the body)

The wall between the refrigerator side and the freezer side in your body is a wall of insulin or sugar. Your body will always hold onto this extra fat until that wall comes down. The only way this wall will come down is fasting. No other diet, a way of exercising, or pill will remove this wall.

This is why we all fail on the new diet. The new exercise plan. The super slimming pill. Initially, it seems like something is happening but 3 to 6 months later we are back to square one. FAIL!

It's a shot to the ego. It gives all your Nah sayers ammunition. It just makes you feel awful. Best of all that you seem to gain weight easier now than ever.

Every low-calorie diet your body will eventually adjust itself to a lower burning level. Your body is smart and will now adjust your daily caloric intake even lower. So now just to sit in one spot for the day you need even fewer calories. Now you eat one slice of pizza and you gain weight. Not fair!

For example, we've all seen the show the biggest loser. On this show, contestants are put on a caloric restriction diet with lots of exercise. It all works for the length of the show. However, we don't get to see the actual results. A year or 2 or 5 later. The participants have gag orders. They aren't allowed to show you where they are now. It's a contract they have signed. Why? Because they have now gained all their weight back. They are back to square one. FAIL! It's not their fault though. It's the facts that are wrong. We have all been told for decades the way to look amazing is to eat small meals throughout the day (5-8 meals) and exercise a lot. Lots of cardio especially.

This formula is all wrong. The body is not tricked by this. Your body in this diet and exercise program simply adjusts its caloric intake. So now what used to be 2500 calories for the day for you now is 1800 calories. Now you gain weight easier than ever! Your body is all about survival. If you were living off the land and you started eating fewer calories than your body will adjust to keep you alive. However, if you were fasting, such as not eating at all for 18 hours then that's where the magic happens. That's where your body says we need to hunt for food: increase muscle, cardiovascular systems, immune system, and cognitive focus. Your body says we are going to need all systems to go.

Fasting and Intermittent Fasting has been done For thousands of years. it's been done sometimes intentional, sometimes it was just what was available. Our bodies as humans evolved to be it's the best health this way. Our bodies are designed to this day to fast. One of the most interesting times in history and fasting for me is the ancient Greeks. They used fasting for brain power. Some of the greatest knowledge came out of Greece during these times.

Plato, the disciple of Socrates, believed in fasting, diet, air, and sun. Sounds like a good recipe to me.

Pythagoras, a Greek philosopher, and mathematician, founder of the famous school of philosophy, would go without food for 40 days and had his students do the same to increase metal perception and creativity.

"Everyone has a physician inside him or her; we just have to help it in its work. The natural healing force within each one of us is the greatest force in getting well. Our food should be our medicine. Our medicine should be our food. But to eat when you are sick is to feed your sickness."
- Hippocrates

"Instead of using medicine, rather, fast a day."
- Plutarch

So you see that this is not a fade. It's not a trick. It's a solid way of living. A way to find happiness, strength, and health. Something sustainable for a lifetime.

One thing Jesus, Buddha, and the prophet Muhammad all agreed on: Fasting.

I'm not asking you to fast for 40 days though. I'm asking you to simply slow down. Give your body a break between digestion. Your body is way more capable than you realize to survive but thrive without food.

I know what you are asking. But won't I waste away? Won't my muscles shrink? Won't I became weak? Won't I be unfocused and groggy?

Short answer no. Long answer no.
You see your body will thrive. All those things you think will happen are all myths. They are all hearsay. They are not true.

My personal experience has been fantastic. I'm in the BEST shape of my life at 40 years old. No, I'm not 25 or 30. I'm 40, a father, work full time, and I own a house(so I'm always fixing something).

Fasting can work for anyone.

Yes, you will get in the best shape of your life… But that's not the best benefits. Prepare to become superhuman. Your immune system will be stronger than ever. Your ailments will suddenly disappear. This has been known to cure diabetes(even type 2). This has been known to prevent and cure cancer. Heart disease. Cure Alzheimer's. Strengthen the cardiovascular system. To extend your lifespan and be healthy, happy and strong all the way through.

I know this seems to good to be true. But I'm telling you, just try it. See for yourself. Look up information on the benefits of fasting. Look up the benefits of wim hof method. It's all there. Are you ready? Let's go. Let's go change the world.

My formula:

it all starts with believing in yourself. You must understand you can and will change. Wim Hof breathing daily. Cold/Hot therapy. Intermittent fasting eating only twice a day lunch and dinner, with good clean farm foods and living water. And a workout plan. I lift weights, with many other activities. But it really can be any workout routine. That's basically it. All summed up into one paragraph. But you must be consistent and persistent. Do this shit every day even if you don't feel like it or it's not your best. Doesn't matter as long as you do it. It's making it a habit.

So why should I believe in myself?

Understand you are your own Superhero. You must be the one to change yourself. No one is going to do the push-ups for you. No one is going to do the meditation for you. No one is going to tell you its time to do your wim hof breathing. No one is going to watch how you eat. It's all up to you and always has been. You create you.
You have all the tools. I know this because I created me! I wasn't born with this information in my head or my body in perfect health. I researched and researched. Tried and failed many many things. But I was persistent. I was hungry. I want the formula for a superhuman, God-like life.

You have all you would ever need and more to complete these goals. The mere fact that you are reading this right now is all the proof you need. You are the one who brought you to this moment in time where this book is in your hand and filling your mind with this life-changing information. Persistent and consistent that's all you need now. Until this becomes a habit. Until this becomes the norm in your life. Just start. Every day for 2 weeks no excuses and it will change your life. In 2 weeks it will become a habit. In 2 weeks it will become the norm. You will begin a transformation like nothing you have ever experienced. You will become one of the most unique people on earth. A person who is of sound mind, body, and soul. A happy, healthy, strong human being. There is no other way for you. It's your time.

What is wim hof breathing and why should I do it?

If you don't know about this, you've been missing out. Wim hof breathing method was invented by Wim Hof a superhuman like man who is from Finland. He discovered putting himself in cold water brought him into the moment completely and made him breathe a certain way. Besides all his world records (climbing Mt Everest in just shorts, running a marathon in the desert with no water, swimming under ice for a long distance) he is much more than this. He has broken all the "facts" inside the medical field. The countless test he has defied all the results. Not only is this amazing, but he has also brought students in of wim hof to achieve the same test results.

So what is so great about this breathing for me?

Doing this breathing resets your body. Like resetting a computer.
 It brings it back to its baseline. If you've ever had your computer not responding well and you restart it you can see how effective this can be. Breathing is chemistry. Your whole body Works on chemistry. The breathing forces oxygen into the parts of the body that are neglected. The breathing raises the pH in your body to more of an alkaline, which is also very beneficial since when we worry and stress we tend to be more acidic in the body.

This alkaline body now allows more neurons from the brain to connect to the body. Giving you a more direct connection to all the systems in the body. To hypothetically allow you to control your body systems by simply thinking about it. Imagine having control over your immune system just like your thermostat on the wall at home. He was able to prove this in the laboratory. Using samples of his blood, they injected him and his students with endotoxin and they were all able to fight it off using their minds. Imagine having this power. It's real. You can have it.
There is absolutely no reason why you can't. One of the worst words in the English language is can't. Every time you hear yourself say can't remember that. It's you forming your life around can't. It's you not believing in you. How the Fuck will you become superhuman with language like that? We all have these abilities. It's just a matter of practice. Persistent and consistent. I will show you how.

Cold/Hot Therapy how to:
This is more about being uncomfortable and facing your fears every day. The advantages to cold exposure daily are off the charts, especially heading fat off the body, creating brown fat on the body(very beneficial). Also, You begin to train an entire group of systems the body barely touches anymore in the modern age. The entire nervous systems. Parasympathetic and sympathetic to be exact. The flight or flight vs the rest and digest. Hitting the cold water to the skin causing the body to react in a strong way, pushes the blood into your organs, cleaning, filtering, regenerating, and strengthening all your vital organs. Your immune system becomes strong and robust. You are now basically lifting weights for your insides.

Let's talk about how to do this. I like to use a sauna and a cold water tub. I find this to be the most effective for me. However, all you really need is a shower, a lake or river, the ocean or any other ways to soak your self (head too) in some cold water.

How cold is cold, I like between 55 and 65 degrees Celsius. I will enter my sauna at 120 degrees for 20 minutes, meditate while in there, then submerge myself in the cold water for 2-5 minutes. Dipping my head all the way under many times. Always be careful in water to feel ok. Blackouts have been known to happen. If you can have a spotter. Especially at first. Then I get out and drip dry. Feeling my back tingle, my body shiver, working the nervous system so well. Then dry off and get dressed. Do not go back into warm water. You want your body to continue strengthening throughout the day. If you feel cold a while later, do some movement snacks, 100 jumping jacks or something.

If you only have a shower you can do many options.
1.   Cold water for the first minute, hot water to soap up and stuff, last minute cold water.
2.   Hot/cold alternate. Go hot water 10 seconds, cold water 20 seconds, for a cycle of 10 times.
3.   Just take cold showers all the time. As you get used to the temp, lower it more, until by the end of the shower you are in quite cold water.

Remember the benefits, especially shedding fat, push yourself to make this a daily routine. This will give you many longevity benefits. You will become a Warrior in no time!

Intermittent Fasting and eating less, I've always been told to eat 6 small meals a day, why is this better?

Yes, I fell for this trap too. For years of my life, I ate 6-8 small meals a day because everything I read on fitness told me this was the way to lean muscle and a great body. FAIL!

Intermittent fasting how to:

It's time to do things the right way. The results way. Break in slow. Get up in the morning and have a cup of decaf tea. I really like peppermint tea. Then I switch over to a bottle of sparkling water. The fizz helps suppress hunger. Then switch to drinking black caffeine coffee. At first, I was just doing this from 6am to 9am then I would eat breakfast. Breakfast. You that's where the origin came from. To break the fast, breakfast.
After a week I would try 6-10. Then before I knew it was easy to make it to noon. So typically I go from 6am to noon for my awake fast. Usually 1 cup of herbal tea upon waking. A bottle of sparkling water. Then around 9am, I will have my first cup of black coffee. Then a second cup around 1030. That's it. It's a great formula for the suppression of hunger and shredded fat. Raising growth hormone. Strengthening your immune system. And feeling focused and great.

This is not the only way. This is not to be followed by the letter. It can be free-flowing. As long as you understand the formula that works. Whatever time you wake is the time to start your awake fast. Then try to make it 4-6 hours before eating. This is the golden time where we shed our extra body weight. This is where the body really thrives. Giving you great focus.

Upon waking
1.   Herbal tea

2. Sparkling water
3. Black coffee

These 3 will help you push through your fast. Try to drinking them in this order. It will work best on many levels.
During your 4-6 hours of awake fasting, this is where the refrigerator and freezer communication beginning. Remember the example of the insulin wall in your body only comes down during nonfeeding. Now your body can use the extra stored in your body for energy.
So instead of eating a meal in the morning, your body simply eats calories from your own storage. Just as filling and rich. Again your body will not break down muscle at all. Not for at least 3 straight days of no good will it even gets close to breaking down muscle to fees the body.

You see your body is designed to survive. We as humans would not be here on earth if our bodies got weaker as we fasted or had a lack of food. Our bodies, in fact, do the opposite, that is we gain strength and focus without eating for short periods such as 16-18 hours without food (dinner to lunch). Your bodies do this naturally because how else would we hunt for food if we just fell down into a fetal position every time 4 hours had passed without food? We again would never have survived.

We become better without feeding constantly. We become stronger through intermittent fasting. We become more focused. We become healthier. We become warriors.

Remember how Powerful you are

No matter what you do in life you are something extraordinary. One of the rules I follow for success is believing in yourself. This is probably the most important rule in life. Nothing else will push you through the tough times better than this. You must understand just how extremely powerful you are as a human being. Such potential. Whatever you put your mind to can and will be a reality if you just focus long enough. But you must be unafraid to fail. You must be able to fall and get back up. Which is another rule, Don't be afraid to fail. Failure is the only way to learn in life. You must understand the valuable lessons in failure. It's the way growth takes place. Watch children. They fail all the time, fall, trip, get hurt. But they get back up. They try again. Until one day the activity becomes effortless.

Now take this program I am presenting and grab it by the balls and lead yourself to victory. Because the greatest thing with a victory is you now have something you can teach others.
 Which is another one of my rules, Give back! Giving back is an equation. The universe works like this. The more you give the more you receive.

For example, I have always found that as I began to train clients or teach a friend about the spirituality book I just read, funny enough I started teaching myself new ways of looking at life. I would get more out of the material I am speaking about than I ever would have gotten without trying to teach someone else these subjects. It sure is interesting how we think life works and how it actually works.
If I've learned anything about the philosophy of life it probably does the opposite of what everyone is telling you to do. See people want you to do what they think. Why Is this? Because people are very insecure in most cases, they all walk around with a voice inside their head saying they aren't good enough. This leads to many qualities in someone's personality like wanting to control all situations or hiding their true selves away from everyone. Yes, it's sad. Because I think it's kind of our right as humans to be able to express our true selves to the world. That's when success happens in these people's lives.
So the reason people want you to do it their way is that if you don't then that makes them question themselves. It hurts there self-identity. They must now consciously of self consciously look at themselves in the mirror and wonder why their way isn't good enough.
It's time for you to gather your answers from within. It's time to find the only answers that ever mattered, yours. Let's see who you are. Let's unlock your full potential. Success is coming. Success is coming big. I want you to repeat that to yourself throughout the day. Just keep saying it. It will start to feel good. It will bring you one step closer to success.

Healthier "YOU" muscle and fat shedding program

Personally, I have tried so many different methods of getting into good physical shape. From p90x, powerlifting, playground training, running, plyometric activities, swimming, cycling, heavy resistance training, split routines, cycle routines, push-pull routines, indoors and out. I have never quieted my passion for studying the body.

I graduated from SUNY Brockport with a physical education degree. With courses like kinesiology, I learned about how the body and muscle movement. When I decided to become a personal trainer, I applied that knowledge to determine how my clients would react to different programs I put them though. The one thing I've found to work the best is my muscle and fat shedding program. And it works for both men and women respectively. With this training, you are getting the most work done in the shortest amount of time. You are focused on form.
 You are pushing the body to gain strength each workout. We are keeping strict records of all our exercises and results. It's the only way to calibrate our workouts to make sure we are becoming true warriors.

The number of hours I have spent in the gym, hiking, running, biking, swimming, playing basketball, track and field, 5k, 10k, climbing, and play a variety of other sports would kill a small horse. I have tried it all to find out what works best for the body, mind, and soul. There is nothing quite like getting a sweat going and a little adrenaline. We were meant to move. We were meant to run. We were meant to compete.

Did I win or have success at everything I did… Hell no. However, I got something more valuable, experience. We undervalue experience. Experience in anything creates knowledge the body, mind, and soul did not have. You can always look back at even failure and learn something. Even if it's… "I'm not going to do that again" lol.
 Always be paying attention always look for the lessons in the world around you. Life is truly your teacher. What I am trying to say in all this is don't be Dogmatic in life. Understand that everything works differently for each individual. That staying strict in anything can lead to dullness, unmotivated, stunted growth bullshit. You must understand consist and persistent are words to live by but you must be willing to try something new. You must be willing to mold yourself around what you have. What are your strengths? What will you have the most success with?

For example, I'm my own life, I live in upstate NY. So I workout by seasons. In the winter I spend most of my time in the gym. I'm the yoga studio. The basketball court. Learning martial arts. Boxing. Indoor stuff. Then when the warm weather rolls around I'll hit the track for some HIIT training. I'll find a playground to do some bodyweight routine. I'll do one my favorites, hiking. I'll go for a nice trail run. Perhaps jump on the bike for some cycling.

So you see just need adaptable. As long as you are getting a workout in 3-4 times a week. Getting the sweat and adrenaline going. Even with all these activities I still focus mostly on molding my body. I love that lean body with the V shape. Wide shoulders and small hips. Hopefully a 6 Pack too. The intermittent fasting really helps with the small waist and 6 pack.

I will be laying out my favorite program for you in the coming chapters.

Chapter 3
Wim hof breathing method: changing the bodies chemistry
"Breathe, Motherfucker"
~ Wim Hof

Disclaimer:
For more Wim Hof https://www.wimhofmethod.com/
The breathing exercises can have strong physiological effects, and must be practiced as instructed. Always perform them in a safe environment, sitting or lying down. Never practice the exercises before or during diving, driving, swimming, taking a bath, or in any other circumstance where loss of consciousness could result in bodily harm. Wim Hof breathing may cause tingling sensations, a ringing in the ears, and/or lightheadedness. These are normal responses and are no cause for alarm. If you faint, however, you have gone too far, and should take it more slowly next time. The cold is a powerful force, and extreme cold can be a shock to your body. We strongly advise to start slow and gradually build up exposure. Always train without forcing anything, and listen to the signals from your body. If not practiced responsibly, there is risk of hypothermia. Do not practice the method during pregnancy, or if you are epileptic.

People with cardiovascular issues, or any other serious health conditions, should always consult a medical professional before starting the Wim Hof Method.

Link to our safety video - https://youtu.be/IFSL_Qk9qKw

What has The Wim Hof breathing method done for me or should I say what hasn't done for me. This method has completely changed my life. For the longest time in my life, I wanted to never get sick. No colds, no bugs, no flu, no cancer, no diabetes, no infections, no nothing. I had a vision of being the healthiest person on earth. This method is the closest thing I have ever found.

The fundamentals:
This breathing technique is a former of a meditation state. While you hold your breath, you begin to change your focus on the outside world to the inside world. You begin to connect to your body in almost a cellular level. You will find great peace in these minutes of no breathing. Your body gets to rest the lungs and the diaphragm. Your body gets to rest the exchange system of oxygen to carbon dioxide. Your body gets to be at peace.
During this time of peace, your body is full of oxygen to all areas, neglected areas. Why does your body have areas that it doesn't get much oxygen? Because we tend to breathe shallowly. Especially under stress. We walk around our daily lives not breathing deep. In a rush. Not focused on the inside.

During this process of the breathing technique, we actually begin to raise our bodies pH level from a hair acidic to a hair alkaline. Being in this alkaline state does wonders. The alkaline state allows more neuron receptors from the brain to connect to the body. Leaving us with a better mind-body connection. In this state, you will start to feel your limbs tingle. Your fingertips and toes especially. Even sometimes your head will also tingle. This is the over oxygenation. This is fantastic for you and really creates miracles. In the more advanced stages, we will use exercise during this period of holding our breath. This will further force oxygen places it doesn't normally reach. You'll be amazed at how much exercise you can do with all that oxygen in your system.
The Wim Hof method as a whole also includes cold water therapy. I, of course, tried this as well as I went through his 10-week course.
Now a year later the only cold water therapy I use on a regular basis is at the end of my shower I turn the water coldish and breath through it until it feels better. The idea behind the cold water is it brings you at the moment. When you get doused with cold water it shocks you. You can't think of anything else. You must be present. The other advantage is it wakes up your immune system. By shocking your body with the cold water it exercises the pores in your skin and your nervous system, thereby strengthening your immune system in the long run. Other than that I didn't stick with the rest of the cold water therapy. It was too uncomfortable for me to want to do it every day.

It's all about adapting to what is sustainable. Consistent and persistent. Modifying what works for us to make us the best us we can be.

Wim Hof breathing method for beginners:
View my step by step video on YouTube:
https://youtu.be/IB2f2nIT2-w
Or search my YouTube channel: Greg's Revolution
Or Go to my website gregsrevolution.com/wimhof

Step 1: find a comfortable spot. A place where you won't be bothered for 30 minutes. This is your time. Your space. Your time for growth and rebirth. No phones, pets, distractions. You owe this to yourself. It's time for a change.

Step 2: get comfortable. You can do this sitting or lay down. You can try it one day sitting and one-day laying, you can actually lay in bed and do this upon waking. I prefer to do this in the fasted or unfed state. I feel I get deeper into it. It's up to your own personal comfort. Remember in this breathing method you may get light headed so just make sure you are safe. Nothing laying around you that could potentially hurt you.

Step 3: take a few deep breaths, just get relaxed. Shut your eyes. Be present. At the moment.

Step 4: begin to breathe in deep and release the breath by just relaxing it out. Do not blow the breath out. Just a relaxed release of breath. Again breath in deep and relax the breath out. Do this 30 times.

If you only make it the first time to 10 or 20 don't panic. You just have to get used to it. This is something new for the body. Give it time.

Step 5: on your final breath in #30 breath in deeper then relax and release the breath almost all the way. Now hold. This is different than going underneath the water in a pool. You usually breathe in and hold. This is a hold with no air in you'd lungs. You'll be very surprised how long you can go without breathing.

Step 6: you're going to notice tingling in your fingertips, ties, head. This is oxygen in areas it doesn't usually get to. This is your body raising its pH level. Just try to be present. Try to travel inside your body and feel it. Notice your heart. Notice your third eye. Notice how your body functions. Talk to it. Tell your body how amazing it is. Thank your body for being so strong and beautiful. Believe me, your body listens. It needs attention. It will begin to improve instantly just from this.

Step 7: as your body starts calling for you to breath again. This can be anywhere from 30 seconds to 2,3,4 minutes. Depending on the person and your experience. You will begin to feel a little panic in your stomach. Your body will say we need to breathe. A tingle like feeling. Try to hold on for another 5 seconds then take a deep breath in and hold. Hold this breath for 10-15 seconds if possible. And exhale all the way.

Step 8: for a few seconds to keep your breath exhaled and feel how good your body feels. Then start the cycle over again. Another 30 breaths of inhaling deep and relax on the exhale. Do this a total of 3 times.

That's it for the beginner stage. It seems simple but what you do inside your body is amazing. This will bring you to almost superhuman potential.
Wim Hof breathing method for Advanced:

2 weeks of doing beginner Wim Hof breathing on a daily basis is time for you to move up to the next step. You will begin with all the same steps you've learned so far in beginners.

Step 9: after your 3 cycles of 30 breaths we want to continue the pattern. On the exhale of your 3rd cycle breath all the way out and hold for a few seconds. Relax and begin another cycle of 30. At the end of the cycle instead of sitting with your breath out of your lungs, you will be doing push-ups. These can be done on your knees if you aren't able to do them the straight legged way.

Step 10: on your 30th breath, breath all the way out and get in push-up position. Without breathing do as many push-ups as possible.

Step 11: when you feel you can not do any more push-ups or must breathe, stop, get back to your seated or laying down position and breath in deep. Hold for a few seconds up to 10 seconds. Your heart will be beating fast.

Step 12:. Now breath normal. Keep your eyes closed. Be inside yourself still. Feel your heart pumping. Now mentally connect to it. Relax it. Slow it down. With each breath, slow the heart.

Step 13: when you have a normal heartbeat. Start another 30 breaths. Breath in deep and relax the breath.

Step 14: when you have done 30 breaths, release your breath then hold for as long as possible. Remember this is about you. About going inside yourself. About connection of mind and body. Be in almost a meditative state.

Step 15: Breath in deep and hold for 10-15 seconds. Now you are done. I like to sometimes just sit for a little bit afterward. Meditate or visualize. I like to visualize my successful self. Finding things I'd like to improve on and seeing myself accomplishing them.

Wim Hof breathing method for experts:

If you have been doing this Wim Hof breathing method for months consistently then congratulations. You are really achieving some things. Your body is thanking you. Now it's time for some tips and tricks to bring you further along on this journey.

Tip 1: At this point begin to play around with breath. Do 30 breaths the first round, then maybe 40 the second and 50 the third. Then go back to 30 on your push-ups round. Then finish your final round with 40. This is just an example. It's up to you. I have done up to as many as 100 breaths. However, for me, it wasn't something I needed to do every day. Just when the mood strikes. Remember don't be Dogmatic. There is a certain freedom in everything. Go with the flow. How your body feels that day. Try new things.

Tip 2: I have found jumping Jacks work better for me then push-ups. I am always breaking my chest down in the weight room so putting all those push-ups in my life just didn't work.
My body was not recovering and healing in time. So I switched to Jumping Jacks. Instead of doing 30-50 push-ups without breathing I am now doing 40-70 jumping Jacks without breathing. The only thing I was worried about was what if I get light headed doing the Jumping Jacks, will I get hurt. Well, they have worked out just fine for me. I experience no problems doing these. Again it's up to the individual.

Tip 3: doing Wim Hof breathing in different environments. My advice is to find different locations to try this. I really enjoy nature doing the breathing. I feel so much more connected to myself and the world. I feel I get deeper. The important thing is you are doing it daily but if you can find a place you are more connected that is a bonus.

Tip 4: cold water therapy. As I mentioned before I do not practice this on a daily basis. The only thing I do in this area is at the end of each shower I turn the temperature down to mild cold and do a round of 30 breaths and 10 seconds of holding after breathing in. Then I will let the water pour on me for another minute before exiting the shower. This little trick stimulus the pours and nervous system. This in turn help strengthen your immune system.

Tip 5: along with the shower I like to get into lakes or pools or some body of water that may be chilly. Let's say a spring or summer morning. Just take a dip. Get chilled a little. Do some breathing. Get back in. Just play with it a little. This is not a routine or a daily activity. Just if the mood strikes to go connect with the body, water, and breath.

Tip 6: over a year of doing the Wim Hof breathing I have really noticed how much my immune system has advanced. How much my cardiovascular system is in shape. How sitting in the silence of no breathing is so meditative. Remember this is about you. This is about being alive and feeling great. Most people in this world are not awake at all. They walk through life not really knowing what being alive means.
You are a very special type of person who is seeking greatness from within and without. Keep focused on who you are as you go through this breathing and how much strength you will gain. As always love thy self. Intermittent Fasting

Chapter 4
Intermittent Fasting
Greg's Revolution way to a lean Herculean body
Eat like a king!

Intermittent fasting has been around for thousands of years in human history. This is nothing new. However, this is a new way of using an old tool. Since the birth of man, we have always discovered new ways of doing things to make our life better and easier. I also have always loved this philosophy. I will always find ways to better my life, to simplify. Kind of like Apple products. Simple smart.

"Simplicity is the ultimate sophistication." — Leonardo da Vinci

Going through so many diets in my lifetime, from low fat, low carb, 6 small meals a day to things like ketosis name of them work or are sustainable for a lifetime. They all take careful planning. They don't allow you to eat freely such as going out to restaurants. They make it hard when you go to other people's houses for dinner to not feel rude. You live out of Tupperware and eat the same bland stuff over and over. Any of this sound familiar?

Intermittent fasting is our answer. There are many ways to do intermittent fasting as well. So whatever fits your lifestyle is the way to go. The idea behind intermittent fasting is to have a feeding window and a non-feeding window. The way I do it is I start my morning usually at 6am. I will only eat twice in one day. Noon and dinnertime. Dinnertime being somewhere between 5-8pm.
If you wanted to follow my blueprint it would be this.

6am- peppermint tea
730am- sparkling water (33oz) probably takes me an hour to drink all that.
9am- black coffee 1cup
1030am- black coffee 1cup
12pm- lunch. Around 1200 calories
3pm- chia tea 1cup with honey and cinnamon
630pm- dinner around 1200 calories

Or

My new routine
Up at 445
Black organic coffee
Go on a run/walk
Hot/Cold Therapy
9am tea(can be any tea)
Rest of morning drink Water (best quality)
12 or 1 lunch variety of veggies, fats, protein, some fruit(best quality)
4 or 5 dinner variety of veggies, fats, protein, some carbs(best quality)
Done eating rest of the night.

That's my daily blueprint. My lunch usually consists of a salad (Dr. Cowan states that our ancestors would graze the lands and pick 15 to 20 varieties of vegetables for a meal, including all parts of plants, roots, seeds, flowers) of local farm quality carrots, parsnips, sprouts, avocado, chia seed, almonds, best quality olive oil, Brazilian nuts, purple potatoes, turmeric, ginger, spinach, Dr. Cowan vegetable powders (www.drcowansgarden.com/#_l_qi), onion, kale, etc. Whatever the farmers market has that week. So you see I try my best to get as much variety in my salad. I usually cook most veggies. Saut or steam. I usually have a side dish of fresh fish, grass fed beef, farm eggs, or beans for protein. Then a fruit.

Dinner is usually different daily but it's veggies, protein oatmeal (I make my own with pea protein), fish, beef, deer, etc. All highest quality. I look for farms that have Raw milk, cheese, and yogurts. Raw is always better.

You really don't have to be super strict with this way of eating because of such a big gap in the non-feeding window but as you see I do try to eat good quality food. It's expensive though. Not impossible. Shopping around for the best prices helps. Farmers markets are the tits. Usually good prices. Local. Full of love.
Join a CSA. Ask the local farmers about it.
In a later chapter I will get more into a food pyramid chart I have created that make way more sense for our health and longevity.
I want you to realize as long as you are consistent, you can make mistakes, eat crap food here an there. The biggest thing is don't eat guilt with it. Enjoy your piece of cake or cookie. Feel the love in it from whoever made it. The last thing you want to do is eat emotions of negativity with your foods. Be grateful.

Also, don't forget your food prayer:
Dear universe, dear mother earth
Dear spirits of this beautiful food
It's with great love and respect I bring you into my being
Would you join me now in mind, body, and soul
So together we can make this world a better place from now into the future
Om… Peace… Amen.

Other ways of intermittent fasting are only eating one meal a day.
Or fasting for 24 hours 2 days a week and eating normally the other days. There are certainly other variations. The reason I fast the way I do is that I'm interested in building lean muscle and strength still. This is the optimal way to do that through intermittent fasting.

If you are on the same goal path as me, of building lean muscle and strength while shedding fat then I suggest following my plan. Now just because I get up at 445am doesn't mean you have to. These are the important things to understand.

Intermittent fasting guidelines:

1. The idea is to have an eating window. From dinner the night before to lunch the next day should be your non-feeding window.
2. Usually, you want to go 6 hours upon waking before eating. So if you get up at 10am then somewhere between 2-4pm would be your first meal. Then maybe 6 hours later is your final meal.

2.   For Beginners don't try to push yourself too far at first. In the beginning, just try to make it an hour or two till your first meal upon waking. Have a bedtime snack. Just slowly break your body and mind into eating fewer times a day and longer gaps. Remember this is something you will be doing for life. That's how Powerful this stuff is. So ease into it. Let yourself adjust. Once you've adjusted you won't even remember you are hungry. Trust me it will sometimes be 2pm and I stop myself and say, wait I didn't eat yet. This is the way we were built. This is how a human being was meant to eat.

3.   Be consistent and persistent. This is a habit you are trying to create in your life. It's going to take some focus and willpower to make this a habit. But like I said, break in slowly. If you are having sugar cravings it's perfectly natural. Include some at the end of your meals. Have a cookie or two. Have a slice of cake. The weight will still keep dropping.

4.   It's the non-feeding window where the magic happens. When you stop eating for 18 hours this is where the magic happens. Your body increases its natural growth hormone.

~Growth Hormone or GH is excellent for your body in healing and growing all muscle and bone. Help repair all cells. Increases protein synthesis. Increases fat breakdown for energy. Balance blood glucose.

During the non-feeding window, your glucose wall drops. If you remember the refrigerator example I gave to you earlier, this is where you can gain access to the freezer or extra storage in the body. Now we can finally use some of our beautifully natural stored energy already in the body. So instead of having 500 calories for breakfast from the cafeteria, you will be dining in and having 500 calories of your bodies natural energy of fat. This is where the fat shedding begins.

Also during the non-feeding window, your brain or cognitive thinking becomes clearer. You actually think better during periods of non-feeding. Like the examples of ancient Greece, I gave earlier. They truly believed intelligence came from fasting.

Other fascinating things about fasting

Fasting is the only thing Jesus, Buddha, and the prophet Muhammad agreed on. They all say great benefits in fasting especially spiritual benefits. Giving your body time to relax from digesting gives it the break it needs to magically heal itself. Whatever the ailments. Just think of your body being able to heal itself every day little by little until it's near perfect. Imagine your immune system so strong you can be sitting in the middle of every sickness but unaffected. Imagine a world where cancer, diabetes, heart disease are very uncommon. This is where I believe intermittent fasting will take us.

Unfortunately, as you may already realize the world we live in is all about the bottom dollar. So, of course, simple things such as baking soda, digestive enzymes, HCl tablets, breathing, and eating less are never suggested by our doctors, never researched by the FDA. Simply because they don't make money.

So we are here to do our own research. We are here to go seek out the people who are pioneering the next wave of being healthy, happy, and strong human beings. People like Dr. Jason Fung, Paul Chek, Dr. Cowan, Ben Greenfield, Ido Portal, Wim Hof. People who teach are things like the Law of attraction, loving ourselves, and breaking the rules to find out who we really truly are.

I follow up that by saying there are very limited studies done, but intermittent fasting or fasting can be used to avoid cancer or even cure it. Some claim 72 hours straight of fasting once per year completely eliminates all bad cells from your body. In turn, eliminates your chances of cancer.
Even more excited is Dr. Jason Fung has already proven to eliminate diabetes type 1 and 2 from people stricken with it just by fasting. Also, he claims to also be able to cure Alzheimer's disease because he believes that is diabetes type 3.
He says Alzheimer's is caused by the gumming up of proteins in the brain. By fasting the body is now able to clear the brain of these protein dams.
So much wonderful health benefits for free!

Please look up all you can on fasting. Learn and absorb. These are two people really pushing the information out.

Check them out on YouTube

Dr. Jason Fung –
Gregory O'gallagher

Chapter 5
The workout:
A plan for one and all for a movie star body

I have spent many years training my body along with my clients. I have watched many personal trainers in the gym training others. Some know what they are doing and some simply suck. Why do they suck, because they usually only know one way to train, that's whatever way they train themselves. For example, I knew a personal trainer who was a powerlifter. He had a powerlifter body, he ate like a powerlifter and he lifted like a powerlifter. I watched as most of his clients were a woman. They were looking to tone and slim down. What program did he put them on? You guessed it, powerlifting. Which of course will do the opposite of their goals. This will make their bodies fatter, heavier, and massive. These people are paying good money for results. They aren't the experts. They don't know the way they are being taught is all wrong for their goals to be met so they do this for a few months. Then after a while with no results they are happy with they quit.

My point being is I have developed a program through my 20+ years experience in personal training and my own development on a program that benefits all body types.

Both men and women. The goal is to shred the body of fat. Make the body stronger and more muscular. To give ample rest time for your body to repair. And to come out the other end looking like a movie star. I mean who doesn't want to walk around looking like the next James Bond or Captain America. The next wonder woman or black widow. This is why my program is called The healthiest "YOU". When you think Hero's', I consider you on the heroes' journey, you think strong, muscular, but lean. You can see his abs. You can see the muscles separation between the shoulders and biceps. The chest and triceps. The quads and hamstrings. Most importantly you are a warrior and a warrior is agile and limber. Can sprint and Dodge. They can balance and climb. They can think clearly and quickly. It's all about being it all. Let's get started!

Let's go in the weight room
Through my years of working out myself and clients, I believe the workout is the least concerning factor.
The diet is the most.
I don't believe you have to work out endless hours or many sets.
I believe in a variety of activities including movement in general.
Movement can be done cleaning the house, gardening, playing with the kids or dog. Just as long as you are moving, in all directions.
Now for a structured program, I present this simple but effective method.
I still believe in having a routine. I still believe that your nervous systems must be pushed with something heavy. So let's get started.

If you have weights at home great! If you have them at a gym that's fine too. Just find a weight set. DO NOT LET YOUR EGO MAKE YOU LIFT MORE THAN YOU CAN HANDLE!

Workout A: Push

Only 20-minute workout
We will be doing 4 push exercises
Use very lightweight. You will be doing these super slow and perfect form. Every exercise to be a count of 5, contraction, hold, and eccentric.
The Squat: Preferably an Olympic bar: Regular squat form, feet shoulder width, back straight, chin up. Down 5...4...3...2...1, hold as low in a squat you can go 5...4...3...2...1, and up 5...4...3...2...1. Remember to breath. Slight pause at the top now backs down. Shoot for 4-7 range. We are only doing one set.
That is all the body needs in slow reps. You draw so much from the nervous system during slow movements, 1 set is sufficient. If the last rep is tough, when you are at the bottom you can try to explode up on the last one just to get that last rep. make sure to keep form.
2. The bench press/chest dip/push up: Any of these will do the trick. It's amazing how hard a 5-second pushup really is. The soreness the next day. Again 5 seconds down, 5 seconds hold, 5 seconds up.
3. Triceps pushdown/close grip bench press/dips: Any of these exercises will do. Again 1 set. 5 seconds slow. Hold at the point of contraction.
4. Shoulder press/military press: 1 set. 5 seconds. Hold at the top.

Workout B: Pull

Again 20 min workout.
3 exercises that pull.
Very lightweight. NO EGO. Super slow with perfect form.
5 seconds contraction, hold at peak of the contraction, and eccentric.
1.   Deadlift/sumo deadlift: Please perfect form here. Look up any YouTube video on deadlift form. Deadlift is maybe the best overall body strengthening exercise. It rocks!
2.   Assisted pull-ups/Lat pulldown/bent over rows: Anyone will do. Change it up once in a while. Remember to stay in the 4-7 range. Perfect form.
3.   Bicep barbell curl/underhand pull-ups/seated dumbbell curl: Choose one. Perfect form. No Swinging weight.

Workout C: Movement

This is freestyle. I promote working on hanging on a bar, squatting as deep as possible with heels on the floor, standing on your head and hands, etc. I also say whatever works for you on any given day. Playing with the kids, dog, cleaning, gardening, etc. Just make sure you are moving.

Workout D: HIIT training

Optional: other alternatives are sports such as basketball, tennis, soccer, football, etc.

Basics of HIIT Training
Sprinting is a great place to be for a shredded muscular body. Also makes us super athletic and explosive.

- Find a field or a track
- Use running sneakers or sprinting sneakers. It is worth investing in a professional fitting
- Athletic clothing, avoid baggy clothes
- A watch or stopwatch

For Beginners - Set Up and Warm Up

- Pick a starting point
- Mark off 30 yards from the starting point. You can do this fairly accurately by walking 30 long strides. You can mark it off as easily as dropping a sweatshirt on the ground at that 30-stride mark.
- Warm up by taking a slow jog. An easy pace will help start blood flowing to your leg muscles
- Jog once or twice around a quarter-mile track or for 2.5-5 minutes around a field. Catch your breath after
- Catch your breath for a few minutes.
- 3 sets of 10 Jumping Jacks.

- Catch your breath for a few minutes

For Beginners – Sprinting, First Leg

1. Stand on the starting line
2. Start the stopwatch
3. Sprint as fast as you can to the 30-yard mark
4. When you reach the 30-yard mark allow yourself to slow down gradually
5. Turn around and lightly jog back
6. As soon as you reach the starting line again, turn immediately around and spirit to the 30-yard mark once again
7. Repeat this 4 times total

For Beginners – Sprinting, Second Leg

1. After you complete the 1st leg, rest for 30 seconds
2. As soon as 30 seconds is up, do jumping squats 6 times at the starting line
3. As soon as you land on the ground after the 6th jumping squat, sprint to the 30-yard mark
4. Walk back to the starting line
5. As soon as you return to the starting line, do another set of 6 jumping squats, then sprint 30 yards again
6. Repeat 4 times total

For Beginners – Sprinting, the Third Leg

1. Return to the starting line after coming to the 2nd leg
2. At the starting line, drop to the ground for 6 clap push-ups or power push-ups.
1. Substitute normal pushups or pushups on the knees if needed
3. As soon as complete, get to your feet and spirit 30 yards.
4. Walk back
5. Repeat for a total of 3 sets

For Beginners – Sprinting, Fourth Leg

1. Return to the starting line after coming to the 2nd leg
1. Do 6 Heisman jumps
2. Immediately sprint 30 yards
3. Walk back
4. Repeat 3 times,

Then:
1. Turn off the stopwatch, jog one-quarter mile to cool down

For Advanced - Set Up and Warm Up

- Pick a starting point

- Mark off 50 yards from the starting point. You can do this fairly accurately by walking 50 long strides. You can mark it off as easily as dropping a sweatshirt on the ground at that 50-stride mark.
- Warm up by taking a slow jog. An easy pace will help start blood flowing to your leg muscles
- Jog once or twice around a quarter-mile track or for 2.5-5 minutes around a field. Then, catch your breath
- Catch your breath for a few minutes.
- 3 sets of 10 Jumping Jacks.
- Catch your breath for a few minutes

.
For Advanced – Sprinting, First Leg

8. Stand on the starting line
9. Start the stopwatch
10. Sprint as fast as you can to the 50-yard mark
11. When you reach the 50-yard mark allow yourself to slow down gradually
12. Turn around and lightly jog back
13. As soon as you reach the starting line again, turn immediately around and spirit to the 50-yard mark once again
14. Repeat this 6 times total

For Beginners – Sprinting, Second Leg

7. After you complete the 1st leg, rest for 30 seconds
8. As soon as 30 seconds is up, do jumping squats 6 times at the starting line

9. As soon as you land on the ground after the 6th jumping squat, sprint to the 50-yard mark
10. Walk back to the starting line
11. As soon as you return to the starting line, do another set of 6 jumping squats, then sprint 50 yards again
12. Repeat 4 times total

For Beginners – Sprinting, the Third Leg

6. Return to the starting line after coming to the 2nd leg
7. At the starting line, drop to the ground for 6 clap push-ups or power push-ups.
8. As soon as complete, get to your feet and spirit 50 yards.
9. Walk back
10. Repeat for a total of 3 sets

For Beginners – Sprinting, Fourth Leg

2. Return to the starting line after coming to the 2nd leg
5. Do 6 Heisman jumps
6. Immediately sprint 50 yards
7. Walk back
8. Repeat 3 times,

Then:
1. Turn off the stopwatch

2. Jog one-quarter mile to cool down

Frequency:

This is tricky because it's going to depend on your body and your diet. The slow pull and push days, it takes some time for the body to be truly ready to push hard in the next workout. So make sure you feel rested and motivated. Write down your results. Try to beat them next workout, without breaking perfect form or 5 seconds.

Later in a chapter, I will discuss recovery. Remember that you DO NOT have to workout everyday or even every week. It's all about feeling your body. What kinds of activities are you doing? Do you have an active job? Are you always chasing the kids around? Do you take daily walks or jogs? Are you walking through the woods many times a week? Are you doing yoga a couple times a week?
All these factor into how you make your specific workout plan. I do encourage to lift heavy here and there. A lot of research has linked heavy lifting on a regular basis to staying younger. As long as you keep your form excellent and slow down!

Chapter 6
The Perfect Formula
"God does not play with dice"
~Einstein

The perfect formula has been laid out for you in a precise plan. It's going to be up to you to be consistent and persistent. This formula will bring you a balanced, healthy, beautiful life. Take your time and be patient in the beginning, it takes time to integrate all this in. To make this stuff a habit. You will see results quickly though once you get going.

Listen to your body, it's always talking to you. Pay attention, it will tell you when it needs a little rest or can be pushed hard. It will give you signs that the immune system is working hard so sitting down and doing some Wim Hof breathing would bring the body just what it needs. Your body will also get stronger and leaner with rest days. As much as we fight it mentally, us gym rats or weekend warriors, who feel like if we skip a workout and everything will go in the shitter. It's just not true. It's our addiction that is telling us that. Our bodies will do just fine with a little rest or hiking, yoga, tai chi, swimming instead of the weight room once in a while.

Always keep yourself fresh and inspired. Find, look, seek your next inspiration. The only life to live is an inspired life.

So as you start this program and start gaining some confidence, start feeling better, go and find athletes you look up to. Go find your heroes. The body types you'd like to be. Go find videos and books they've written. Absorb information. Absorb motivation. Keep yourself focused on your goals.

For a side note, I am always working towards learning and growing. I'm never satisfied with what I know, I want to know more. Learning is a process until the day I leave earth. I surround myself with motivation. Listening to speakers such as Les Brown, Eckhart Tolle. Podcast such as Bruce Lee(daughter), Mind Pump, Ben Greenfield, Revolution Radio Fitness Podcast!. I listen about the law of attraction. I listen to people who think outside of the box. Who believe that life is about making an impact on others. Inspiring others. It's very important to grow constantly. No matter what your circumstances you are able to rise. Tough situations have an equal and opposite seed of growth in the positive you just have to find it.

Let's me quote one of my favorite famous people The Rock. "Just bring it".
The man with a non-stop motor who is always so motivated and inspiring to others. He believes in early rising to bring success. He is up at 4am most mornings getting his workout in.

Go find nature… Get in touch with nature. Meditate in nature. Walk in nature. Bathe in nature. It's been here long before us and perhaps long after us. Respect what it can tell you. How nature can make you feel. It's always in the moment. It's always full of life. Especially in the spring and summer.

Understand that walking around barefoot on the soil and grass is a connection to mother earth. I know it's very hippie of me but it's true. Some say the connection to earth like that can balance your body. The earth knows exactly what you need.

If you can, connect with your family. Your family will be with you most of your life. Keep them close because you will need each other in tough moments of life. I'm over to my parent's house weekly. My sister has two kids and I have one.
I try to get them together as much as possible. Teaching my son the value of family. It wasn't too long ago we all traveled and lived in tribes. The roots of tribes are strong because of the family/community aspects. Depending on each other as a pack to survive and thrive.

Whatever gender you are don't be afraid to try things like yoga, martial arts, and even trampolines. All these activities bring different forms of strength and flexibility. Giving your mind and body new things to learn and calibrate to, brings new neuron connection from mind to muscle.

The combination of Wim Hof breathing, hot/cold therapy and Intermittent Fasting is going to be an excellent 1-2-3 punch for your being as a whole. There are so many benefits. Pumping your body full of oxygen, the absolute stillness inside yourself during the non-breathing phase, the energy rush of both methods, boosting your immune system, increasing your stamina, reduce stress on all aspects, decreased risk of major disease, an act of loving yourself, becoming a lean, muscular superhuman, and much more.

Discipline is one of the important lessons in life. This workout program I've created, it encourages lots of discipline. This will spill over into your life In many aspects. You will become better at setting goals for yourself and accomplishing them. Think big, but set small goals to keep you on the path with rewards. Learning to write down your accomplishments in the workouts and go try to beat them the next time will show you how to do this on a daily basis I'm your own life. Being successful in one area of your life will teach you how to be in all.

Chapter 7
Spirituality

"Health is a state of complete harmony of the body, mind, and spirit. When one is free from physical disabilities and mental distractions, the gates to the soul open."
~B.K.S. Iyengar

Stress in your life is the number one problem in this fast-paced world, and we lack healthy coping mechanisms. High-stress levels eventually lead to increased cortisol levels in the body. The side effects of long-term high cortisol levels are alarming:

- Increased body fat
- Mood swings
- Reduced sex drive
- High blood sugar
- Unstable metabolism
- Hypertension
- Suppressed immune system
- Broken sleep
- Anxiety

These conditions all can lead to chronic illness. Being under high stress all the time is slowly but surely killing you. Physical ailments caused by prolonged stress are bad enough; even worse I believe
that stress often changes your mindset and leads you to miss out on happiness. You are missing out on experiencing all life has to offer.

  Death is not the sad part; the sad part is that some people will go through their entire lives barely living at all. I encourage you to live. I want you to open your eyes; both the physical eyes and the third eye. Become aware of the world around you and all the wonderful things you walk right by every day and are blind to. You are missing out on a lifetime of experiences as unique as your fingerprints that nothing can ever duplicate.

So many of us know this intuitively, but we maintain our daily rituals feeling that we do not have time or energy to make a change. Instead of reducing stress, we find addictive behaviors to cope. We overeat, drink excessive alcohol, smoke tobacco, and act promiscuously.

We walk around like zombies, filling our coffee cups to the brim, spilling it as we try to get it to our desks and meetings. A half-cup is never enough; in excess is the only thing that comforts us at that moment.

We know, deep down inside, there is more to life. We feel oppressed, lonely, separated, and judged. Chemical and behavioral coping mechanisms soothe us temporarily.

But the human experience is supposed to be a holistic experience of mind, body, and spirit. We the people of the united world are missing the point of living. We no longer pay attention to Mother Nature and what she teaches. We have stopped feeling our internal spirituality. We forget that we are a miracle. We live on a supposed spinning orb, the invisible force of gravity to keeping us on the surface, next to a 10,000-degree star, floating in space that may be endless, to the best of our knowledge.

We are missing the point, when we are concerned with being on time or late, making the boss mad, stressing over disagreements with another person, or simple car trouble. I am not telling you these things cannot be part of your life, as I too stress about these things once in a while. What I am suggesting is to examine stressors in a new way. Step back from the situation and watch as an outsider. Find trust in yourself and the universe that you are exactly where you need to be, at precisely the right time. Life will always work it is way out one way or the other.

Mother Nature does so much for the psyche if you allow her to. Let the wind blow you, let the steam carry you, let the sun warm you, let the rain cleanse you. Notice that nature works so effortlessly. Observe puffy white dandelion. Catch one blowing in the wind. Hold it in your fingertips.
The dandelion seeds move around like it is alive and trying to escape. But it cannot, it is just a flower and cannot squirm and fight. This is the beauty of nature, that dandelion needs to expel no energy to move, it uses nature's wind to guide it. We can learn a lot from this example.

We have been taught over and over that everything takes extreme effort and excessive amounts of hard work. Take for example a rowboat. We use all our efforts and energy to get across the lake with paddles. It works but it takes much effort and the boat does not travel far all that quickly. Thinking outside the box, we discovered that nature has a gift for us - the wind. We put a sail up and our boat is moved with very little effort on our part. This is working smarter, not harder. Let nature guide you in working smarter.

Let's think outside the box all the time. Unfortunately, we really limit our abilities because we do not think this way. When we realize this and start practicing thinking outside the box, we can do incredible things. Even better, we make this world a better place because thinking holistically we no longer feel incomplete. Fear dissipates inside of us, eliminating those all so common emotions of anxiety, jealousy, envy, anger, and the need to be right. With all those emotions watered down, a balanced, healthy you and the world prevails.

Conflict

Why is there so much conflict in the world? Because challenging the beliefs that someone else holds dear causes that person to doubt themselves.   Doubt begets fear; fear begets the urge to fight. An example ongoing for centuries is religious conflict.

One society challenge another's beliefs on god; the resulting doubt and fear cause a holy war. Societies will continue to fight in vain, attempting to confirm other societies to their beliefs. We need to stop trying to preach to people against their will. Instead, we need to focus on ourselves and build from the inside out. If you are truly holistic you will not even blink at someone who challenges your beliefs. You will understand from the heart that another's opinion of your beliefs truly does not matter. We are all having a human experience. Through the human experience, everyone is as unique as a fingerprint and we are all in search of who we are. The freedom of allowing your neighbors to be whoever they choose to be is freeing yourself in the highest of respects. I want you to realize the more you focus on something, the more you give it attention, the more you war against something, the stronger it gets and it ends nothing.

Trust in yourself

Feeling trust in yourself is very rewarding as is finding your answers from within.

Trusting in your intuition is a process that does not happen overnight. As you need to learn to trust a new person, you need to learn to trust yourself. Keep in mind that your intuition will lead you places that you may think this is wrong, but have confidence that you are right where you need to be. You must sometimes learn, see, and be in unfamiliar places before you can arrive at your destination. Keep in mind it is the journey, not the destination that brings happiness.

Alignment

In order to start using your intuition, you want to find something called alignment. The idea of alignment is to settle mindset of feeling happy, good, confident, grateful, aware, relaxed, and/or connected to yourself. There are many ways of doing this. For each person, it will be a little different. For some people, it is music that helps. For another, it is listening to an inspiring speaker, exercising, or spending time with your pets.
Take time to find yours. Once you have found it, do it daily, especially in the morning. This will set forth a great start to your day as we set forth our intentions for the day in the morning. This is a very important step to changing your life for the better. You'll be amazed at how differently your day will go when you are in alignment.

Creating your happiest life and living your dreams

We are trained by pleasing the people around us. We are conditioned to please others, often trying to please an invisible man. We do not even realize how it is now our natural instinct to keep those around us happy while focusing on ourselves last. Take the time to evaluate how much time you spend pleasing others, and notice what others are doing as well. Do others seem happy, or are they suffering inside, suffocating their burning fire inside of them? Once you determine that you do in fact spend more energy on others' happiness than your own, decide to change your methods.

Without judgment, allow others to keep themselves happy in their own way, and begin finding thoughts and habits that feel good to you instead of ones that please others. It is your job to figure out who you are, not who they are. Focus on yourself!

When you focus on yourself and find things that make you happy, ask yourself why you want that thing. Envision having that thing that makes you happy, be it a feeling or an object. Start small, so that it is believable to you. Imagine how your life changes and the emotions associated with having it. When we feel emotions, it engages our nervous system and becomes physical to us and can now become an action to take. You will unknowingly begin the steps to obtaining that idea or object. A simple example of this is that perhaps I am getting hungry for lunch. I have a thought what I want because it will taste good and cure my hunger, making me happy. I decide I want a hamburger. I have just created thought of my lunch. It will not magically appear. I must stay focused and continue to want this lunch and feel it is the perfect lunch for me.

I thought and created my lunch in my mind, and I had an emotional response to enjoying how that creation feels to me. Then my nervous system was engaged, which made it physical. Now I go to my freezer, get the burger out with the bacon and begin creating that very lunch I pictured. This thought did not exist one hour ago until I created it with thought. I bet your nervous system was working too, just picturing my lunch. This is a very superficial example, but the concept is useful. Engage your thoughts on what makes you and only you happy and content, and with practice, you can create a perfectly happy life for yourself.

You are unstoppable if you believe in yourself and find your strength from within. Practice the green light system in life. Say yes at every opportunity. Do not anticipate failure; go for whatever you imagine will make you happy.
Every situation, "good" or "bad" is about expansion. The expansion is one of the basic purposes of life. Every experience that you have is a success! Change your perspective on the ideas of success and failure. The journey itself is a success.
It is the journey, not the destination that brings us happiness. The absolute outcome is not as important as your expansion through the experience. Say yes to challenges, relationships, a new job, or spontaneous road trips. Say yes to breaking some rules!

Just go!
Just live!
Just breathe!
Just expand!

Use your thoughts and words to create a new world to live in. It is that simple. It just takes focus. It just takes wanting to live the green light life. Using wisdom instead of chaos to get things done in your life. Take the time in the morning to focus, meditate, build the momentum of positive success for the day.

If you are picky about what car you drive, clothes you wear, or what phone you have, start being picky about what you think. Try to have focused thoughts that will bring you an abundance of whatever it is you want from life.

 I mentioned earlier you can learn a lot from Mother Nature. Mother Nature is abundant. Look everywhere. Fields full of flowers. You could not even count them all. Beaches of endless sand, forests of endless trees, oceans of endless water cover the globe. Mother Earth sure understands abundance. We can be abundant too. Whatever you want money, food, relationships, fun, laughter, or health, everything is all in front of us. Do not let your thoughts tell you otherwise. You have been conditioned to think this life is limited and it is a fallacy. The truth is that you create limitations for yourself by how you think. Change your thoughts. Understand the world is so abundant. Money is a physical representation of our work. It is formed from energy. Energy is infinite. Money is just another way people rick or lacking. I am using money as my example because it seems to be a big one among everyday people. We've attached many ideas and judgments to money. People with money are selfish or out of touch. People lacking money are lazy or careless. These again are all conditions we have been taught. Breakaway. Change your thinking. Think with wisdom. Strip down stigmas you have attached to your ingrained ideas of the world. Open new doorways for yourself. Do not pay attention to what other people are doing. Instead, concentrate on you and focus your life.

I also want you to understand grinding away on a problem to get to a solution, is not the way you solve it. And it is not living; rather it is focusing on the problem and giving it too much attention. It is a sickness in and of itself. We have to learn to relax and let everything fall into place. If you focus on what you want, have fun along the way and enjoy the journey, things work out. It is amazing how many doors open when you just let go and relax. Just look, feel, see, and be fun, like you were when you were a carefree child.

Awaken to your new holistic life
Awaken to your new thriving life
Awaken to your new balanced life
Awaken to your new life of wisdom
Awaken to working smarter, not harder
Awaken to your new understanding of energy
Awaken to your new life of positive momentum

Service to others

One of the greatest ways to make your own happiness is through service to others. We as human beings are built in this way. It is why raising our children even on a difficult day with them is rewarding. Everything in the human body wants us to be kind, serve others who serve us. Service to others is instilled in us so deep that our emotional bodies are directly connected to the action. We cannot help ourselves but want to do something for someone who does something for us. We radiate positive energy when we genuinely and altruistically help others. If there is an agenda attached to the action it spoils the meaning and negates the positive energy. We have lost many of these concepts in the modern economy. We have begun to ignore the human system of giving, trading and connecting with each other to achieve a task. Whenever you can, buy a coffee for your neighbor, co-worker, a stranger with no expectations. Help someone without asking them if they need help, just help them. Talk to people to get to know them, giving them your undivided attention. This is all service to others. You will immediately feel your momentum pushing forward, your soul expanding because this is how we were built.

Fear and lies

Most of us have fears that we are not even aware of until we are faced with triggering situations. Or, we are desperately afraid of feeling like we do not belong. So we lie to people and ourselves because of an instinct for survival. We do this constantly, it is a habit. We tell white lies all day. Take on a challenge of sorts: for a two-day period, try not to tell one lie, no matter how insignificant or small. You will be amazed at how much you catch yourself telling small lies to get through everyday situations. I'm not telling you this is a bad thing; I just want you to be aware of who you truly are. By telling the truth you reveal parts of yourself that you normally hide.
Take the time to comprehend these elements of yourself as they may be completely novel. The more truthful and open with yourself you are the more expansion can happen. If you realize what lies you tell, you can realize your truths. I also want you to realize that by simply telling the truth, you will find new opportunities that were not previously obvious.

For example, you will find learning opportunities if you finally tell your boss that you do not understand something and need training. Another example is asking questions. We tend not to ask very many questions, again trying to save face, or appear smarter than we feel. Asking questions creates interpersonal connections, between speakers and listeners. By asking the speaker questions you bring a new way of teaching to the speaker. Then for anyone else involved in the conversation also brings them clarity and confidence to ask their own questions and brings together people on the same wavelength and creates a tribe. It is winning for everyone.

Patience and discipline

Your behaviors were not developed overnight. It will take focus and effort to get unburied from current habits and thoughts and develop new ways of thinking. It is taken me almost a decade of practice. Martial arts teach discipline and discipline is a definite help with this stuff too. Discipline sounds like a bad thing. In reality, it is just bringing structure to your practice so that you can stay focused on where you want to go in life. Use your imaginary sword to cut away all the self-doubt and pity. All those thoughts do nothing for you. You must go beyond them and find unconditional self-love. For a lot of people, this is such a hard concept. The majority of clients I have guided through a self-love meditation come out crying, almost uncontrolled sobbing. We do not realize how many dams we build inside ourselves to block and deny ourselves love and therein lies the difficulty. Have patience with yourself and enjoy the process.

You and you alone are the only things over which you will ever have control. Learn to accept that you do not have control over what happens to you, whether or not you get what you desire, or even whether you hear bad news. Anyway, you are exceptional, extraordinary, and you are a miracle.

Never surrender your dreams.
Like an artist, decorate your canvas.
Like a farmer, prepare your fields for rain.

Like a master, flow effortlessly through movement

Finding Freedom
It's well known that we live by imaginary rules made up by imaginary people to keep us following the path of imaginary expectations. Be brave and step out of this box. Open that mind up as wide as possible. Be something you never thought you could be, complexly free! As an exercise start becoming comfortable with no clothes on. Free yourself to who your ancestors were so long ago. Be comfortable in your own skin.
 Eventually find a place you can be in nature completely, extraordinarily, shamelessly naked. Even better is to skinny dip in a lake. This is You! This is natural and normal. The lesson is to understand all the shame you have been taught, all the covering up, was all bullshit. It is not offensive in any way. This is compiled you! The shift in your mind after this experience is nothing short of amazing.

Chapter 8
Rest & Recovery
"Chi is the commander of blood and blood is the commander of chi"
~ Greg's Revolution

Many ways to rest and recover. Sleeping, meditation, yoga, sauna, tai chi, swimming, breathe work, walking, hiking, canoeing, kayaking, even lovemaking are all examples.

Meditation is one of the most important ways to unlock your potential in my opinion. It has taught me where true confidence comes from. It has given me my voice. It has centered me and shown me the path from the physical world to the beyond. I owe so much of my last 20 years to meditation.
These 2 meditations are easy followed along journeys. Please try both with an open heart.

Meditation Energy Balance:
https://gregsrevolution.com/meditation1/

Meditation Sacred Heart:
https://gregsrevolution.com/sacredheart/

Besides Meditation take up tai chi, yoga, walking in nature barefoot, swimming, cuddling with a loved one…
Or

The most perfect recharge and balance for a human being because we are in fact a biological battery is to be walking on a beach barefoot, with the sun out, the ocean waves bringing salt into the air and you holding hands with the love of your life. Makes you feel great just thinking about it.

Listen to your intuition. Listen to your body. Don't be stubborn. You will know when you are fully recovered and ready to go to the next level. Until then just rest and recover. As you see that is not just sitting on the coach. It being active in recovery.

The last checks and balance you can do are wear a heart rate and heart rate variability monitor. You can wear one full time or just strap it on upon waking in the morning. This will give you a great idea of how your day will go. This will show you how your heart is balanced by the nervous systems. It will tell if you are ready to be a beast today or time to recover. Use this tool as your guidance.

Chapter 9
Define your dream
"When the student is ready the master appears, even if its written on a wall from 100 years ago"
~ Paul Chek

It's time for you to adopt the habit that got me to where I am today. This is perhaps the most important activity in this whole book. It's time to define your dream. What is it that you are here on this earth to do? I want you to brain storm and set your dream. Tell me in this space I have left in this book on the next page, what is your 3-5-year plan. What do you hope to accomplish? After you have written this down, I want you to write down what you will do in this present moment to start the momentum going in that direction. I want you to set yourself several small goals. One by one I want you to feel the emotion in them. I want you to envision yourself accomplishing these goals and how that is making you feel. Put all 5 senses into feeling these goals accomplished. Everything you do from now until the day you reach your dream, I want you to step back and evaluate does this bring me closer to my dream or further away. This will keep you on course and keep that arrow pointing in the right direction!

What is your dream?

_____

_____

_____

_____

_____

_____

_____

_____

_____

_____

_____

What goals will bring you closer to this dream?

Reread your dream for many weeks. Start completing some of your goals. Make them small steps so you can check them off. Make sure you are evaluating the decisions in your daily life that they are bringing you closer to your dream. Even if you work a job you don't like but it's bringing you closer to your dream, that is completely alright. It's time to achieve your dreams, now!

Do my meditations, they will also help you get closer to your dream. The subconscious mind is very powerful.

Chapter 10
Let get real about Food choices
"A co-creator in the universe with GOD, you have to experience whatever you create"
~Paul Chek

Lets get real!

The Real Food Pyramid

Healthy fats — 3-5 servings
Coconut oil, meat, flakes. Olive oil. Macadamia nut oil. Avocados. Olives. Organic grass fed butter. Organic yogurt. Ghee. Free range whole eggs. Cod liver oil. Raw nuts. Raw seeds. Wild fish. Almond butter. Flax oil. Bacon. Mayonnaise. Dark chocolate.

Vegetables — 3-5 servings
Avocados. Kale. Sweet potato. Swiss chard. Fermented veggies. Broccoli. Asparagus. Sprouts. Olives. Cauliflower. Cabbage. Bok choy. Collards. Yams. Corn. Potatoes. Peas. Carrots. Radish. Arugula. Squash. Zucchini. Lettuce. Fennel. Plantains. Spinach.

Proteins — 2-4 servings
Free Range full eggs. Wild fish. Organic pure protein powders. Organic yogurt. Pasture raised organic beef, bison, buffalo, pork. Miso, tamari, tempeh, natto. Soaked or sprouted beans and legumes. Raw seed and nuts. Raw milk and goat milk. Raw cheese.

Carbs — 1-2 servings
Wild rice. Brown or white rice. Soaked organic quinoa. Oats. Hemp cereal. Gluten free oats. Sprouted beans and legumes.

Fruits — 1-2 servings
Apples. Grapefruit. Berries. Bananas. Cherries. Apricot. Watermelon. Lemons. Limes. Figs. Natural dried fruit. Strawberries. Dates. Papayas. Nectarines. Oranges. Pears. Pineapple. Mangoes. Kiwi. Plums.

Spices — As needed
Cinnamon. Garlic. Ginger. Turmeric.

As you can see I have a whole different idea about what is a proper food chart. We have been steered all wrong and it's time to right the ship. There are so many "diets" out there. Believe me I have tried many. Vegan, Keto, many small meals, carb loading, low fat, and on and on. The fact is they can all be used at proper times. They are just tools in the tool chest. You don't build your dream home with just a hammer. You end up using the hammer at the proper times, the drill, the saw, etc. When it makes sense. So, if I just get done deadlifting, well for the next couple days I will be extra hungry. I will crave more protein such as animal flesh. After a few days I can almost eat vegan until I hit it hard again at the gym.

I even used the vegan diet for 9 months to filter my system out. I felt refreshed after that journey. I also learned so much about myself and my taste buds. It literally changed my life experience forever.

So, what does this new improved food pyramid chart mean for you?

Well first, it shows you to not be scared of fat! Fats are really good for you. Make fats your priority. Introduce more and more into your diet.

Second, is get all the veggies you can into your diet. Try to get a little bit of everything in your salads. Using Dr. Cowans powders and microgreens like the awesome ones from Saratoga Urban Farms (who were on the podcast Revolution Radio), variety becomes much easier.

Third, do not cut out all carbs from your diet. I do not think this is the long-term answer. I think by intermittent fasting, the carbs become less of a problem to the body. You need some carbs. Nothing to the extreme usually becomes beneficial in the long run.
Fourth, have fun with this food pyramid. Try new foods. Try to widen your taste buds. Join an olive oil club, find a great dark chocolate distributor, go to a farmer's market and meet awesome growers!

I encourage you to find the best salts. Himalayan pink salt, Celtic salts are some of the best. They have fantastic minerals in them and are the opposite of table salt.
They are actually really good for you. Especially finding the right source.
Remember it's all about your sources. That's why I try to shop local. Finding farms nearby. Raw milk farms, Meat farms, farmers markets, co-ops. If you look closely enough you can feel the energy in the food. You can see the people who sell this stuff and how much they love doing it. It all goes back to loving ourselves enough to give ourselves the right kind of food. It doesn't have to be expensive. Just a different source.
And remember to respect your food, without it you would not be alive. Say your food prayer from the earlier chapter.

Conclusion
"Life itself, when understood and utilized for what it is, is sweet."
~ Benjamin Hoff

It is said that even before a river falls into the ocean it trembles with fear. It looks back at the journey, through the mountain peaks, the winding path through the forest, past the people, and it sees in front of it such a vast ocean that entering into it is nothing but disappearing forever. But, there is no other way to go. The river cannot go back from where it came and neither can you. You can only go forward. The river simply has to take the risk of going into the ocean. And only when it enters the ocean will the fear disappear, because only then will the river know it is not disappearing, rather, it is becoming one with the ocean. Through the balancing and strengthening of all three aspects of what makes you, mind, body, and soul, you will become complete and perhaps one of the most unique people on earth, ahead of your time, or part of the future people of this planet. Each experience will push the boundaries of the universe. The universe is learning about itself through us. We are unique as a fingerprint. We are extraordinary beings.

Throughout my years of personal training and at the same time awakening in my own way, I saw the absolute need to focus on the whole being instead of just the physical part. I started to understand that people are not complete, people are broken. The good news is it can be fixed. Not only by getting a beach body or a healthy-looking body but also through personal training the inside parts of a human being. Through gaining wisdom, open-mindedness, and learning to love one's self. These are so important to happiness. The healthiest "YOU" program has one big goal and that is to bring you the tools to bring happiness, health, and strength to you for life. The perspective you gain will carry you through hard times and keep you aware of all the great lessons around you.

Having a diet which you understand the science behind is something that I think most people can stick with. When you understand the meaning behind a practice, it is amazing how easily the habits can be adopted.

We live in a chaotic media-driven world telling us what is good and bad for us when what we really want is an understanding of why, while most of the time we never find an answer. That why I back this diet so firmly. I do not even like calling it a diet; it is a lifestyle. It is no longer feeling sleeplessness over indigestion. It is no longer having undigested food in your stomach, rotting and causing illness and pain. It is no longer experiencing energy highs and lows. Personally, I have never felt healthier or happier intermittent fasting after decades of discomfort and sickness. Friends, family, and even doctors could not determine the root cause of my symptoms and over-the-counter medicines could not heal me. I became so frustrated I started researching how digestion progresses biologically and I finally found understanding.

A very powerful personal tool for this program is being consistent. Consistency leaves room for error. You can have a bad workout, shallow meditation, or eat poorly for a day, but as long as you're consistent and persistent you will experience success with this program in the short term and especially the long term.

Any further questions you can contact me through my website https://gregsrevolution.com

And of course, keep looking out for more podcast, articles, meditations, and other useful life gems! I am also available as a coach in person or online https://gregsrevolution.com/coaching

Thank you all from the bottom of my heart
Namaste
~Greg